Date: 10/5/15

J BIO TROUT
Anderson, Jameson.
Mike Trout /

MIKE TROUT

Awesome Athletes

thrive

Checkerboard Library

An Imprint of Abdo Publishing
www.abdopublishing.com

Jameson Anderson

www.abdopublishing.com

Published by Abdo Publishing, a division of ABDO, PO Box 398166, Minneapolis, Minnesota 55439. Copyright © 2015 by Abdo Consulting Group, Inc. International copyrights reserved in all countries. No part of this book may be reproduced in any form without written permission from the publisher. Checkerboard Library™ is a trademark and logo of Abdo Publishing.

Printed in the United States of America, North Mankato, Minnesota.
052014
092014

THIS BOOK CONTAINS
RECYCLED MATERIALS

Cover Photo: Getty Images
Interior Photos: AP Images pp. 7, 11, 13, 17, 21, 23, 25, 29; Corbis pp. 26, 27; Getty Images pp. 1, 5, 9, 15, 19, 24–25

Series Coordinator: Tamara L. Britton
Editors: Tamara L. Britton, Megan M. Gunderson
Art Direction: Neil Klinepier

Library of Congress Cataloging-in-Publication Data

Anderson, Jameson.
 Mike Trout / Jameson Anderson.
    pages cm. -- (Awesome athletes)
 Includes index.
 ISBN 978-1-62403-336-0
1. Trout, Mike, 1991---Juvenile literature. 2. Baseball players--United States--Biography--Juvenile literature. I. Title.
 GV865.T73A64 2015
 796.357092--dc23
 [B]
                          2014002722

TABLE OF CONTENTS

THE CATCH

June 27, 2012, was a sunny day at Camden Yards in Baltimore, Maryland. Los Angeles Angels of Anaheim center fielder Mike Trout had grown up in nearby New Jersey. Trout's family and school friends were there to see him play. His parents sat in the stands along the third base line.

In the bottom of the first inning, Orioles **shortstop** J.J. Hardy stepped into the batter's box. Trout could tell all the way outfield that Hardy was swinging for the center field fence. Hardy connected with a **breaking ball** tossed by Angels pitcher Jered Weaver. As the ball left Hardy's bat, it looked like a home run.

As the ball approached the fence, Trout jumped as high as he could and opened his glove. When he landed, his teammate Torii Hunter told him to check his glove. Trout did, and the ball was there! He had robbed Hardy of a home run.

In addition to The Catch, Trout scored three runs and had one RBI.
The Angels defeated the Orioles 13–1.

Fans of both teams cheered Trout's awesome catch. Trout could hardly believe it. He turned and watched the replay on the stadium's giant screen. It was the first time he had robbed an opposing player of a home run. But it would not be the last.

HIGHLIGHT REEL

Michael Nelson Trout was born in Vineland, New Jersey.

1991

Baseball America named Trout its minor league Player of the Year.

2011

Trout once again played in the All-Star Game, and once again came in second in MVP voting; Millville Senior High renamed its baseball field Mike Trout Field.

2013

2009

Trout was drafted by the Los Angeles Angels of Anaheim.

2012

Trout was named American League Rookie of the Year; he played in his first All-Star Game; he came in second in league MVP voting.

2014

The Angels signed Trout to a six-year, $144.5 million contract.

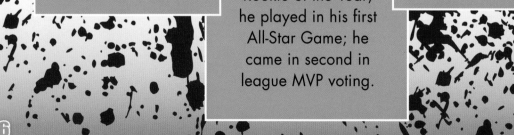

MIKE TROUT

DOB: August 7, 1991
Ht: 6'2"
Wt: 230
Position: CF
Number: 27
Bats: Right
Throws: Right

CAREER STATISTICS:

Batting Avg:	.314
HR:	62
RBIs:	196

AWARDS:

All-Star: 2012, 2013
Rookie of the Year: 2012
Silver Slugger Award: 2012, 2013

BORN TO BASEBALL

Michael Nelson Trout was born on August 7, 1991, in Vineland, New Jersey. His parents are Jeff and Debbie Trout. Mike has an older brother, Tyler, and an older sister, Teal.

Mike's father also played baseball. In 1982, he was **drafted** by the Minnesota Twins. He played in the team's **minor league** system for four years. Jeff had to quit when he injured his knee. He returned to Millville, New Jersey. There, he became a history teacher and coach.

As a young boy, Mike's father coached both football and baseball at Millville High School. Mike often helped out Thunderbolt teams. By age 6, Mike was the baseball team's official ball boy. He ran to get balls that players missed during practice. During games, he carried water to the players.

Mike began to develop baseball skills at a young age. He also had the patience it would take to play the game.

Some kids became bored standing in the outfield or sitting in the **dugout**. But not Mike! He loved to play and watch the game.

At 9 years old, Mike's Little League coach Mike Kavanagh said Mike was one of the best kids on the team. And he was playing on a team of 12-year-olds!

The patience Mike developed as a young man would be an important part of his major league success.

420

HIGH SCHOOL STAR

By the time he entered Millville Senior High School, Mike was a great fielder. He also played **shortstop**, and he could pitch too. He ran bases with amazing speed for a player his age. He was timed at less than 4 seconds from home plate to first base!

During his junior year, Mike pitched a **no-hitter**. That year, the Thunderbolts played in the New Jersey state tournament. The Thunderbolts advanced to face the Cherry Hill East Cougars in the championship game.

The Cougars coaches knew that to win, they would have to stop Mike's powerful bat. To that end, the Cougars intentionally **walked** Mike every time he came to the plate.

Mike was walked when the bases were loaded, giving the Thunderbolts a free run. The Cougars walked Mike even when Mike represented a winning run. The Thunderbolts could not counter this strategy, and the Cougars took the win.

Mike's speed would be a key factor in his Major League Baseball success. In 2012, he became the first rookie in MLB history to hit 30 home runs and steal 40 bases.

THE MOVE OUTFIELD

Mike spent his summer vacations improving his game. While other kids traveled or stayed home and played video games, Mike attended baseball tournaments. In this way, he demonstrated his skills to **scouts** around the country.

By his senior year, Mike had proven he could handle the fast pace of the **shortstop** position. Because of his speed, Mike's coaches thought he could easily chase down fly balls in the outfield. So, they moved him to center field.

The move to the outfield didn't hurt Mike's hitting. He continued to knock balls out of the park when he was up to bat. During his senior year, Mike hit 18 home runs. It was a New Jersey state high school record!

Mike would be the first player in MLB history to get at least 45 steals, 30 home runs, and 125 runs on his way to being named Rookie of the Year.

FUN FACT MIKE WAS SO FAST THAT HE WAS CALLED THE MILLVILLE METEOR.

THE PLAN FOR THE FUTURE

Mike wanted to play **Major League Baseball (MLB)**. But he also knew college was important. Because of his high school **statistics**, a number of colleges were interested in Mike. Mike accepted a **scholarship** from East Carolina University.

Though Mike was accepted to college, he still dreamed of being **drafted** by a major league team. **Scouts** from a number of teams had come to watch Mike's high school games. They took notes and compared Mike to other young players. It was up to the scouts to help their teams decide which players to draft.

Mike made a connection with Greg Morhardt from the Los Angeles Angels of Anaheim. Morhardt had

FUN FACT AS A HIGH SCHOOL SENIOR, MIKE BATTED .531, SCORED 49 RUNS, HIT 45 RBIS, STOLE 19 BASES, AND TOOK THE STATE RECORD WITH 18 HOME RUNS.

been a teammate of Mike's father in the **minor leagues**.
Morhardt rated Mike as the highest-ranked non-pitcher he
had ever seen.

Morhardt decided that Mike was his first choice. **Scouts**
from other teams still visited Mike. But Mike and his family
hoped that the Angels would select him on **draft** day.

The East Carolina University Pirates baseball team has made 26 NCAA
tournament appearances.

DRAFT DAY

The 2009 **Major League Baseball Draft** began on June 9, 2009. Mike wasn't sure which team would select him. The Angels had picks 24 and 25 in the first round. Some experts expected that Mike would go earlier in the draft.

However, sometimes players from colder climates are not drafted as early as predicted. Players in warm climates such as Florida or California can play baseball all year long. But in colder climates such as Minnesota or New Jersey, players can only play baseball during the spring and summer months.

Perhaps because of these concerns, Mike was still available when the Angels made their selections. The Angels chose Mike with their 25th pick. Mike had realized his dream of being drafted by a professional team. But he knew it would take a lot of work to make it through the **minors** and into the big leagues.

FUN FACT SAN FRANCISCO 49ERS QUARTERBACK COLIN KAEPERNICK WAS ALSO TAKEN IN THE 2009 MLB DRAFT. THE CHICAGO CUBS SELECTED HIM WITH THE 1,310TH PICK IN ROUND 43.

Major League Baseball commissioner Bud Selig *(left)* congratulates Mike after his selection in the MLB draft.

THE MINORS

Trout played 39 games for the Rookie-level Arizona Angels. He often played **shortstop**. During his first game, Trout reached base six times! While with the Arizona Angels, Trout was at bat 164 times. He hit .360 with 1 home run. He also knocked in 25 RBIs and had 13 stolen bases.

His great performance with the Arizona Angels brought him a promotion to Class A ball. He finished out the 2009 season with the Cedar Rapids Kernels.

Trout began his second season with the Kernels. That year, he averaged an amazing .362. He had 113 hits and 6 home runs in 312 trips to the plate.

At just 19 years old, Trout was named *Baseball America*'s **minor league** Player of the Year. He was the youngest player to receive the award.

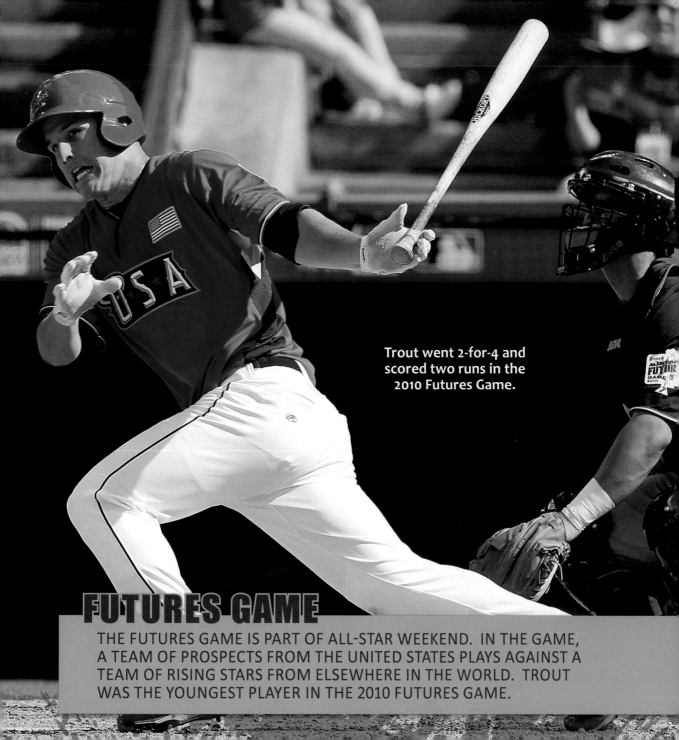

Trout went 2-for-4 and scored two runs in the 2010 Futures Game.

FUTURES GAME

THE FUTURES GAME IS PART OF ALL-STAR WEEKEND. IN THE GAME, A TEAM OF PROSPECTS FROM THE UNITED STATES PLAYS AGAINST A TEAM OF RISING STARS FROM ELSEWHERE IN THE WORLD. TROUT WAS THE YOUNGEST PLAYER IN THE 2010 FUTURES GAME.

Trout quickly advanced in the **minor leagues**. He spent the remainder of the 2010 season with the Class A Advanced Rancho Cucamonga Quakes. His **batting average** remained high, as he slugged .306 in 196 at-bats. He had 60 hits and 4 home runs. He scored 30 runs of his own, while hitting 19 RBIs.

Trout started 2011 in Double-A with the Arkansas Travelers. He hit .326 in 353 at-bats. His 115 hits included 11 home runs. He was safe at home 82 times, and batted in an additional 38 runs. Trout was known as baseball's best prospect.

MINOR LEAGUE BASEBALL

MiLB IS DIVIDED INTO SIX CLASSES

Triple-A
Double-A
Class A Advanced
Class A
Class A Short Season
Rookie

Players begin in the Rookie class and advance as their play improves.

Midway through the season, Trout received the call he had been waiting for. The Los Angeles Angels of Anaheim called him up to the **major leagues**. But Trout struggled in the big show. He worked to get used to major league pitching. After just 12 games, the Angels sent Trout back to the Arkansas Travelers.

Trout wasn't discouraged. He thanked the Angels fans and coaches for the fun he had in Anaheim and vowed to work harder in the **minors**.

Trout dives for a ball during a game against the Baltimore Orioles. He hit a home run in the bottom of the eighth inning and the Angels won the game 8–3.

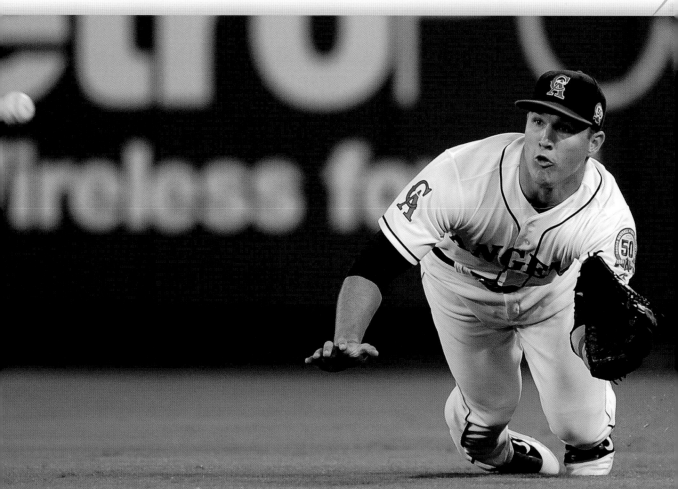

MAJOR LEAGUE

Trout started the 2012 season in Triple-A with the Salt Lake Bees. He averaged an incredible .403 at the plate. He had 31 hits, batted in 13 runs, and had 1 home run.

But Trout played only 20 games with the Bees. That April, the Angels called him back up to Anaheim. Now Trout would show fans how good he could be.

In what was officially his **Major League Baseball** rookie season, Trout hit .326. He scored 129 runs on 182 hits. He had 83 RBIs and used his amazing speed to steal 49 bases.

Trout's performance earned him a trip to the 2012 **All-Star Game**. He won the **Silver Slugger Award**. He was named American League (AL) Rookie of the Year. He just missed the Most Valuable Player (MVP) Award, coming in second to Detroit Tiger Miguel Cabrera.

Trout gets a hit in the 2012 All-Star Game. The NL All-Stars beat the AL All-Stars 8–0.

Trout continued his amazing performance in 2013. He went to the plate 589 times, getting 190 hits and batting in 97 runners. He scored 109 runs, the most in the AL. Twenty-seven of those were homers. And, he picked up 33 stolen bases. Trout earned another **All-Star Game** appearance. Again, he finished second behind Miguel Cabrera for AL MVP.

On August 30, 2013, the Angels played the Brewers in Milwaukee. Shortstop Jean Segura caught Trout stealing at second and tagged him out, but the Angels won the game 5–0.

In 2013, 10 of the 11 home runs Trout hit traveled more than 408 feet (124 m). On May 23, Trout hit this home run in the first inning against the Kansas City Royals. It flew 463 feet (141 m)!

Trout is the first player with less than three years of MLB service to sign a contract worth more than $20 million a year.

Going into the 2014 season, Trout was considered to be the best all-around player in **Major League Baseball**. But he earned only $510,000. Many fans did not believe this was a fair amount for Trout's achievements.

On February 26, 2014, Trout and the Angels agreed to a record-breaking one-year contract worth $1 million. Two days later, Trout hit a **grand slam** and drove in five runs in a pre-season game against the Chicago Cubs!

But the Angels wanted to make certain that Trout would not sign with another team. On March 20, 2014, Trout agreed to a $144.5 million contract. The deal will keep Trout with the team through 2020.

Trout got one hit and scored one run in two at-bats in a 12–9 win over the Chicago White Sox on May 18, 2013.

LOOKING AHEAD

In addition to his contributions on the field, Trout also gives to his community. He volunteers to visit area schools. There, he and other Angels talk to kids about the importance of staying in school.

In 2013, Trout donated money to repair the batting cages and the field at his high school in Millville. The money was part of the bonus he received from the Angels when he was named AL Rookie of the Year. Because of Trout's generosity, the baseball field at Millville Senior High School was renamed Mike Trout Field.

Mike Trout will be a free agent in 2021. No matter where he plays, Trout has the skills to be a great player. He has a long career ahead of him.

Trout is a fan favorite at Angel Stadium of Anaheim.

GLOSSARY

All-Star Game - a game between the American League All-Stars and the National League All-Stars.

batting average - the number of hits a batter gets divided by the number of the batter's at-bats.

breaking ball - a pitch that does not travel toward a batter in a straight line, but moves sideways or downward.

draft - an event during which sports teams choose new players. Choosing new players is known as drafting them.

dugout - the seating area for team members who are not currently on the playing field.

grand slam - a home run that is hit when there are runners on all three bases. A grand slam scores four runs.

Major League Baseball (MLB) - the highest level of professional baseball. It is made up of the American League and the National League. It is also called the majors.

Minor League Baseball - the five classes of professional baseball that are lower level than the major leagues. It is also called the minors.

no-hitter - a game in which one team does not get any hits. This is difficult for a pitcher to achieve.

scholarship - money or aid given to help a student continue his or her studies.

scout - a person who evaluates the talent of amateur athletes to determine if they would have success in the pros.

shortstop - a player who defends the area between second and third base.

Silver Slugger Award - an award given each year to the best offensive player at each position in the American League and the National League.

statistics - numbers that represent pieces of information about a game. Hits, strikeouts, runs, and batting average are a few of a baseball player's statistics.

walk - when a pitcher causes a batter to go to first base by pitching four balls outside the strike zone.

To learn more about Awesome Athletes, visit **booklinks.abdopublishing.com**. These links are routinely monitored and updated to provide the most current information available.

INDEX